Accelerated Christian Training Series

Laying the FOUNDATION

BOOK 3

A CALL TO FAITH AND OBEDIENCE

Dr. Mark Hanby

Destiny Image® Publishers, Inc.
P.O. Box 310
Shippensburg, PA 17257-0310

"Speaking to the Purposes of God for This
Generation and for the Generations to Come"

ISBN 0-7684-2144-6

For Worldwide Distribution
Printed in the U.S.A.

This book and all other Destiny Image, Revival Press,
MercyPlace, Fresh Bread, Destiny Image Fiction,
and Treasure House books are available
at Christian bookstores and distributors worldwide.

For a U.S. bookstore nearest you, call **1-800-722-6774**.
For more information on foreign distributors,
call **717-532-3040**.
Or reach us on the Internet: **www.destinyimage.com**

Contents

Introduction

And you shall know the truth, and the truth shall make you free (John 8:32).

What Is Truth?

Truth Is a Person

"What is truth?" Pilate asked Jesus (Jn. 18:38). The answer to Pilate's timeless question was standing before him. Truth is not a series of facts or the sum of information. Truth is a Person: Jesus Christ. Jesus said of Himself, "I am the way, the truth, and the life" (Jn. 14:6). Truth is not only rational, it is relational. Religious theory that only teaches about God can never liberate the soul. True freedom is found in knowing Him. "And ye shall know the truth, and the truth shall make you free" (Jn. 8:32).

God has chosen to unfold His relational truth in various ways throughout the Bible and always in the form of personal relationship between Himself and men such as Adam, Noah, and Abraham. The unfolding revelation of God's relationship with man was spelled out in agreements between God and man called covenants. What better way to unfold a relational truth than in the context of relationship?

Truth Is the Result of Seeking Jesus

This relational truth is more than experience. Despite his great experience on the road to Damascus, the apostle Paul did not end his search for truth but wrote, "...that I may know *Him* and the power of His resurrection, and the fellowship of His sufferings..." (Phil. 3:10, emphasis mine). Job, wounded and in distress, cried out, "Oh that I knew where I might find *Him...*"

(Job 23:3). Jesus said, "Blessed are those who hunger and thirst for righteousness, for they shall be filled" (Mt. 5:6). Our finding the truth is the result of a hunger to know the Person of Jesus Christ. We do not seek truth and find Jesus; we seek Jesus and find the truth.

Truth Is a Highway

We may think of truth as a highway—an endless journey into the Person of God. All of us walking in the light of relationship with God are at some point in that journey. As we "seek the Lord" and "search the Scriptures," we advance. The **A**ccelerated **C**hristian **T**raining **S**eries has been created to help us move on in that journey into the Lord regardless of whether we are new believers or seasoned saints of God. There is always more truth for us regardless of our place along the road. "His ways [are] past finding out" (Rom. 11:33b).

It is important that every believer follow a course such as this. Although the believer may be exposed to a variety of good biblical preaching, there must be a systematic seeking after truth to provide a foundation upon which to grow in relationship with the Person of Jesus. Imagine agreeing to marry someone of whom you had only seen a pencil sketching. It is our intention in this course of seeking to paint a full and vital portrait of the Christ who is alive in you.

If you are a new traveler on the highway of truth, you have begun the most exciting journey of your life. Many parallels can be drawn between the new believer and a newborn child. It would be a criminal act to leave an infant out in the cold or in a house without someone to give him attention and care. It is likewise a tragedy when the Church does not nurture newborn Christians. If newborns are going to be healthy and grow to maturity, they must be carefully and loving fed with the truth of the word.

Truth Brings Maturity

The Christian life is a "growing up into Him in all things...until we come to the measure of the stature of the fullness of Christ" (see Eph. 4:13-15). It is important that we place ourselves under pastoral care if we are to "grow up." Even Jesus, who astonished the doctors and lawyers of His time, was entrusted to His parents' care. The Bible says, "Obey thse who rule over you, and be submissive: for they watch out for your souls" (Heb. 13:17). To reject the care of pastoral oversight is to reject God's plan to bring us to Himself and to leave ourselves open to error and the exit from the highway of our journey into the truth.

The ministry that God has given to the Church is five-phased with a threefold purpose. Ephesians 4:11 tells us that God has placed in the church apostles, prophets, evangelists, pastors and teachers. Their purpose is to mature, feed and motivate believers in their own calling and ministry. Only when this equipping is established in the life of the believer will they progress from spiritual newborn to spiritual childhood and on to spiritual adulthood.

In the life of every Christian there must come a point where we "put away childish things" (1 Cor. 13:11). As we become "rooted and grounded" in the basic principles of faith we are "no more children, tossed to and fro, and carried about with every wind of doctrine" (Eph. 4:14). As we grow and mature in the faith we are able to rise above our own problems and trials and reach out with power and confidence to minister the truth to the needs of those around us.

How the Accelerated Christian Training Series Works

The **A**ccelerated **C**hristian **T**raining **S**eries has been designed to meet the crucial need for intensive training in the basic doctrines of the Christian faith. These doctrines are revealed in the context of relationship between God and man. It is designed as a self-instruction course in which believers can journey at their own pace. You will find review questions at the end of each section of material you have studied that will help you to retain what you've learned.

There is an exercise called "Dig a Little Deeper; Grow a Little Closer" at the end of each major section. These reflective questions are designed to help you synthesize the truths you have been taught and then apply them in a personal way. You will be invited to journal throughout the study of this book to provide you with a record of your new understanding and growth in God. Journaling will help you to grow in your ability to hear God's voice and adjust your life and understanding to His purpose.

Following this **A.C.T.S.** course will stimulate and accelerate your spiritual understanding and bring you to a more intimate knowledge of the Truth, who is Jesus Christ. We pray that you will grow in the awareness of the Lord's presence as He guides you to Himself through the study of His Word.

Two Companions for the Road

During this time of new growth in your spiritual life there will be questions that come to mind. You will meet two companions throughout this series on the road to truth. They are Newly Newborn and Truly Taughtright. Newly will ask some of the same questions that you ask, and Truly, his mentor, will give the answers.

A Call to Faith and Obedience

As we consider what we have learned so far about the relationship between God and man, there are two words which loom large in biblical accounts: *faith* and *obedience*. Faith is another word for trust. In the very beginning Adam and Eve enjoyed an intimate life with God. God would come to fellowship with them in the "cool of the day." This was a time of communion between Creator and creation. Because man knew his God in this intimate relationship there was never a separation of purpose between God and Adam. Adam believed (had faith in) God and in so doing stayed in this living and righteous relationship with Him.

When satan slithered into the picture, he brought with him the very opposite of trust and obedience. He brought doubt and rebellion. The righteous relationship between man and God was broken as man chose to believe the serpent's lie that God was holding out on him. Without faith/trust and obedience there could be no intimacy between God and Adam.

How was this rift to be settled? The only way to restore this living relationship was to restore trust and obedience. In the story of Abraham and his descendants we will see the beginning of God's calling man back into this relationship of trust and obedience.

As you read through the material in this section, it would be good to read and memorize these Scriptures. Keep them in mind as we see how God began to restore this relationship of trust and obedience.

> ...Abraham *"believed God, and it was accounted to him for righteousness"* (Galatians 3:6).

> *But without faith it is impossible to please Him, for he who comes to God must believe that He is, and that He is a rewarder of those who diligently seek Him* (Hebrews 11:6).

I. Abraham: The Father of Faith and Obedience

A. Who Was Abraham?

1. Abraham was a man called into relationship with God.

Now the Lord had said to Abram: "Get out of your country, from your family and from your father's house, to a land that I will show you" (Genesis 12:1).

Look to Abraham your father, and to Sarah who bore you; for I called him alone, and blessed him and increased him (Isaiah 51:2).

And he said, "Brethren and fathers, listen: The God of glory appeared to our father Abraham when he was in Mesopotamia, before he dwelt in Haran, and said to him, 'Get out of your country and from your relatives, and come to a land that I will show you'" (Acts 7:2-3).

2.   Abraham was a man who believed God.

And he believed in the Lord, and He accounted it to him for righteousness (Genesis 15:6).

For what does the Scripture say? "Abraham believed God, and it was accounted to him for righteousness" (Romans 4:3).

...Abraham "believed God, and it was accounted to him for righteousness" (Galatians 3:6).

By faith Abraham obeyed when he was called to go out to the place which he would receive as an inheritance. And he went out, not knowing where he was going (Hebrews 11:8).

3.   Abraham was a man who obeyed God.

In your seed all the nations of the earth shall be blessed, because you have obeyed My voice (Genesis 22:18).

...Abraham obeyed My voice and kept My charge, My commandments, My statutes, and My laws (Genesis 26:5).

4.   Abraham was called a "friend of God" who walked in intimate fellowship with God.

Are You not our God, who drove out the inhabitants of this land before Your people Israel, and gave it to the descendants of Abraham Your friend forever? (2 Chronicles 20:7)

But you, Israel, are My servant, Jacob whom I have chosen, the descendants of Abraham My friend (Isaiah 41:8).

And the Scripture was fulfilled which says, "Abraham believed God, and it was accounted to him for righteousness." And he was called the friend of God (James 2:23).

5.   Abraham was the father of all who inherit the promises of God by faith.

As for Me, behold, My covenant is with you, and you shall be a father of many nations (Genesis 17:4).

Therefore it is of faith that it might be according to grace, so that the promise might be sure to all the seed, not only to those who are of the law, but also to those who are of the faith of Abraham, who is the father of us all...He did not waver at the promise of God through unbelief, but was strengthened in faith, giving glory to God, and being fully convinced that what He had promised He was also able to perform (Romans 4:16,20-21).

B.   What Did God Promise to Abraham?

1.   God promised to make Abraham a great nation.

2.   God promised to bless Abraham.

3.   God promised to make Abraham's name great.

4.   God promised to make Abraham a blessing.

5.   God promised to bless those who blessed Abraham.

6.   God promised to curse those who cursed Abraham.

7.   God promised to bless all the families of the earth through Abraham.

I will make you a great nation; I will bless you and make your name great; and you shall be a blessing. I will bless those who bless you, and I will curse him who curses you; and in you all the families of the earth shall be blessed (Genesis 12:2-3).

8.   God promised to give the land to Abraham's descendants.

Then the Lord appeared to Abram and said, "To your descendants I will give this land." And there he built an altar to the Lord, who had appeared to him (Genesis 12:7).

For all the land which you see I give to you and your descendants forever (Genesis 13:15).

9.   God promised that Abraham's descendants would be numerous.

And I will make your descendants as the dust of the earth; so that if a man could number the dust of the earth, then your descendants also could be numbered (Genesis 13:16).

Then He brought him outside and said, "Look now toward heaven, and count the stars if you are able to number them." And He said to him, "So shall your descendants be" (Genesis 15:5).

Blessing I will bless you, and multiplying I will multiply your descendants as the stars of the heaven and as the sand which is on the seashore; and your descendants shall possess the gate of their enemies (Genesis 22:17).

10.   God promised that Abraham would be the father of many nations.

As for Me, behold, My covenant is with you, and you shall be a father of many nations. No longer shall your name be called Abram, but your name shall be Abraham; for I have made you a father of many nations (Genesis 17:4-5).

Since Abraham shall surely become a great and mighty nation, and all the nations of the earth shall be blessed in him? (Genesis 18:18)

11.   God promised that kings would be in Abraham's line.

I will make you exceedingly fruitful; and I will make nations of you, and kings shall come from you (Genesis 17:6).

And I will bless her and also give you a son by her; then I will bless her, and she shall be a mother of nations; kings of peoples shall be from her (Genesis 17:16).

12. God promised victory to Abraham against his enemies.

Blessing I will bless you, and multiplying I will multiply your descendants as the stars of the heaven and as the sand which is on the seashore; and your descendants shall possess the gate of their enemies (Genesis 22:17).

C. What Did God Require of Abraham?

Genesis 12:1 says, *"Now the Lord had said to Abram"*:

1. God required Abraham to leave his country.

"Get out of your country..."

2. God required Abraham to leave his family.

"from your family..."

3. God required Abraham to leave his father's house.

"and from your father's house..."

4. God required Abraham to go to a land He would show him.

"to a land that I will show you...."

Abraham's total dependence would now be upon God, not what was familiar, comfortable or dependent upon human effort.

God was pleased with Abraham's trust and obedience.

D. What Is a Covenant?

1. A covenant is an agreement that binds two or more parties to each other in relationship. Each party agrees to fulfill certain conditions and each enjoys advantages as a result.

2. In covenant both parties agree on the terms and conditions for agreement. An example would be the marriage covenant or an employment contract.

E. How Did God Make a Covenant With Abraham?

1. God made a covenant with Abraham in which He set forth all the terms and bound Himself to fulfill the covenant.

After these things the word of the Lord came to Abram in a vision, saying, "Do not be afraid, Abram. I am your shield, your exceedingly great reward." But Abram said, "Lord God, what will You give me, seeing I go childless, and the heir of my house is Eliezer of Damascus?" Then Abram said, "Look, You have given me no offspring; indeed one born in my house is my heir!" And behold, the word of the Lord came to him, saying, "This one shall not be your heir, but one who will come from your own body shall be your heir." Then He brought him outside and said, "Look now toward heaven, and count the stars if you are able to number them." And He said to him, "So shall your descendants be." And he believed in the Lord, and He accounted it to him for righteousness. Then He said to him, "I am the Lord, who brought you out of Ur of the Chaldeans, to give you this land to inherit it" (Genesis 15:1-7).

2. God established the terms of the covenant with Abraham. God is superior to man and therefore God sets forth the terms. Man must choose to either accept or reject God's offer.

3. God guaranteed the covenant with the shedding of animal blood, which represented an exchanging of life.

For the life of the flesh is in the blood (Leviticus 17:11a).

And he said, "Lord God, how shall I know that I will inherit it?" So He said to him, "Bring Me a three-year-old heifer, a three-year-old female goat, a three-year-old ram, a turtledove, and a young pigeon." Then he brought all these to Him and cut them in two, down the middle, and placed each piece opposite the other; but he did not cut the birds in two. And when the vultures came down on the carcasses, Abram drove them away. Now when the sun was going down, a deep sleep fell upon Abram; and behold, horror and great darkness fell upon him (Genesis 15:8-12).

For when God made a promise to Abraham, because He could swear by no one greater, He swore by Himself, saying, "Surely blessing I will bless you, and multiplying I will multiply you" (Hebrews 6:13-14).

4. God required the sign of circumcision of Abraham to demonstrate that he had accepted God's offer of covenant relationship. This included all Abraham's sons, male servants, and all other men who wanted to work for Abraham.

And God said to Abraham: "As for you, you shall keep My covenant, you and your descendants after you throughout their generations. This is My covenant which you shall keep, between Me and you and your descendants after you: Every male child among you shall be circumcised; and you shall be circumcised in the flesh of your foreskins, and it shall be a sign of the covenant between Me and you" (Genesis 17:9-11).

5. Those who did not accept this sign of covenant relationship were to be excluded from the life of God's people. They had refused God's offer of covenant relationship.

And the uncircumcised male child, who is not circumcised in the flesh of his foreskin, that person shall be cut off from his people; he has broken My covenant (Genesis 17:14).

F. How Did Abraham Demonstrate His Acceptance of God's Offer of Covenant Relationship?

1. Abraham demonstrated his acceptance by believing God. He took Him at His word and lived according to God's covenant terms. This we call faith.

And he believed in the Lord, and He accounted it to him for righteousness (Genesis 15:6).

2. Abraham demonstrated his acceptance by obeying God and going into the land God had promised him.

By faith Abraham obeyed when he was called to go out to the place which he would receive as an inheritance. And he went out, not knowing where he was going. By faith he dwelt in the land of promise as in a foreign country, dwelling in tents with Isaac and Jacob, the heirs with him of the same promise; for he waited for the city which has foundations, whose builder and maker is God (Hebrews 11:8-10).

3.   Abraham demonstrated his acceptance even in offering back to God what was most precious to him, his own son Isaac.

By faith Abraham, when he was tested, offered up Isaac, and he who had received the promises offered up his only begotten son, of whom it was said, "In Isaac your seed shall be called," concluding that God was able to raise him up, even from the dead, from which he also received him in a figurative sense (Hebrews 11:17-19).

G.   How Did God's Covenant Continue After Abraham?

1.   The covenant and blessings of God continued through Abraham's son Isaac. Isaac was a child born to Abraham and Sarah his wife after they were too old to have children.

"And I will bless her and also give you a son by her; then I will bless her, and she shall be a mother of nations; kings of peoples shall be from her." Then Abraham fell on his face and laughed, and said in his heart, "Shall a child be born to a man who is one hundred years old? And shall Sarah, who is ninety years old, bear a child?" (Genesis 17:16-17).

2.   Isaac received the covenant sign of circumcision as required by God.

Then Abraham circumcised his son Isaac when he was eight days old, as God had commanded him (Genesis 21:4).

Then He gave him the covenant of circumcision; and so Abraham begot Isaac and circumcised him on the eighth day; and Isaac begot Jacob, and Jacob begot the twelve patriarchs (Acts 7:8).

3.   God appeared to Isaac and confirmed the covenant and the promises.

And the Lord appeared to him the same night and said, "I am the God of your father Abraham; do not fear, for I am with you. I will bless you and multiply your descendants for My servant Abraham's sake" (Genesis 26:24).

H.   How Did God's Covenant Continue After Isaac?

1.   God's covenant continued through Jacob, the son of Isaac.

Now Isaac pleaded with the Lord for his wife, because she was barren; and the Lord granted his plea, and Rebekah his wife conceived. But the children struggled together within her; and she said, "If all is well, why am I like this?" So she went to inquire of the Lord. And the Lord said to her: "Two nations are in your womb, two peoples shall be separated from your body; one people shall be stronger than the other, and the older shall serve the younger"...Afterward his brother came out, and his hand took hold of Esau's heel; so his name was called Jacob. Isaac was sixty years old when she bore them (Genesis 25:21-23, 26).

2.   God chose Jacob to receive the covenant blessing even though he was not the oldest son. It is up to God to choose whom He will use to bring about His purposes.

And not only this, but when Rebecca also had conceived by one man, even by our father Isaac (for the children not yet being born, nor having done any good or evil, that the purpose of God according to election might stand, not of works but of Him who calls), it was said to her, "The older shall serve the younger" (Romans 9:10-12).

And when there had been much dispute, Peter rose up and said to them: "Men and brethren, you know that a good while ago God chose among us, that by my mouth the Gentiles should hear the word of the gospel and believe" (Acts 15:7).

3.   Jacob received the covenant blessing from his father Isaac.

Then Isaac called Jacob and blessed him, and charged him, and said to him: "You shall not take a wife from the daughters of Canaan...May God Almighty bless you, and make you fruitful and multiply you, that you may be an assembly of peoples; and give you the blessing of Abraham, to you and your descendants with you, that you may inherit the land in which you are a stranger, which God gave to Abraham" (Genesis 28:1,3-4).

4. God changed Jacob's name to "Israel," and Israel became the father of twelve tribes who were called the "children of Israel."

Then Jacob was left alone; and a Man wrestled with him until the breaking of day...And He said, "Let Me go, for the day breaks." But he said, "I will not let You go unless You bless me!" So He said to him, "What is your name?" And he said, "Jacob." And He said, "Your name shall no longer be called Jacob, but Israel; for you have struggled with God and with men, and have prevailed"...And Jacob called the name of the place Peniel: "For I have seen God face to face, and my life is preserved" (Genesis 32:24,26-28,30).

Let's Review What We Have Learned About Abraham and Covenant Relationship.

1. Abraham _____ God and it was accounted to him as righteousness.

2. Abraham was called a "_____ of God" who walked in intimate fellowship with God.

3. Abraham was the father of all who inherit the
_____ of God by _____.

4. A Covenant is an _____ that binds two or
more parties to each other in _____.

5. In Genesis 15, God guaranteed the covenant with the shedding of _____, which represented an exchanging of
_____.

6. Abraham's total _____ would now be upon God,
not what was _____, _____ or dependent
upon human effort.

7. Name three of the blessings that God promised to Abraham in Genesis 12.

_____

_____

_____

8. God required the sign of _____ of Abraham to
demonstrate that he had _____ God's offer of
covenant relationship.

9. In a few words, why was it a miracle that Isaac was born?

_____

_____

_____

10. _____ received the covenant blessing from his
father Isaac.

11. Jacob's name was changed to _____.

Dig a Little Deeper; Grow a Little Closer

1. Read the following text and respond to the questions below.

> *The Lord said to Abram, "Leave your country, your relatives, and your father's home, and go to a land that I am going to show you"* (Genesis 12:1 TEV).

2. As we study the Scriptures we discover that Abraham was the son of an idol maker in the ancient land of Ur. (See Joshua 24:2.) What was it that God was really challenging Abraham to do in this passage of Scripture? What did he have to leave behind in order to pursue God?

_____

_____

_____

_____

3. What things are you and I going to leave behind as we obey God? Prayerfully consider here what things might be holding you back from a fuller relationship with God. Write your thoughts here.

_____

_____

_____

_____

Review Notes

Abraham: The Father of Faith and Obedience

Abraham: The Father of Faith and Obedience

_____

_____

_____

_____

_____

_____

_____

_____

_____

_____

_____

_____

_____

_____

_____

_____

_____

_____

_____

_____

_____

_____

Abraham: The Father of Faith and Obedience

Abraham: The Father of Faith and Obedience

Abraham: The Father of Faith and Obedience

_____

_____

_____

_____

_____

_____

_____

_____

_____

_____

_____

_____

_____

_____

_____

_____

_____

_____

_____

_____

_____

_____

_____

_____

_____

_____

_____

Abraham: The Father of Faith and Obedience

Abraham: The Father of Faith and Obedience

II. Israel, Called to Be the People of God

A. Who Was the Nation of Israel?

1. The children of Israel grew into the nation of Israel while they lived in the land of Egypt for over 400 years.

Then He said to Abram: "Know certainly that your descendants will be strangers in a land that is not theirs, and will serve them, and they will afflict them four hundred years. And also the nation whom they serve I will judge; afterward they shall come out with great possessions" (Genesis 15:13-14).

But the children of Israel were fruitful and increased abundantly, multiplied and grew exceedingly mighty; and the land was filled with them (Exodus 1:7).

2. The nation of Israel was God's people who were persecuted in Egypt.

Now it happened in the process of time that the king of Egypt died. Then the children of Israel groaned because of the bondage, and they cried out; and their cry came up to God because of the bondage (Exodus 2:23).

3. God wanted to continue His covenant with the nation of Israel by bringing them into what He had promised to Abraham.

So God heard their groaning, and God remembered His covenant with Abraham, with Isaac, and with Jacob. And God looked upon the children

of Israel, and God acknowledged them (Exodus
2:24-25).

4.   God chose Moses to lead Israel out of the
        bondage of Egypt and into a theocracy
        under God. (Theocracy—the rule of God.)

*Moreover He said, "I am the God of your father—
the God of Abraham, the God of Isaac, and the
God of Jacob." And Moses hid his face, for he was
afraid to look upon God..."So I have come down to
deliver them out of the hand of the Egyptians, and
to bring them up from that land to a good and
large land, to a land flowing with milk and honey,
to the place of the Canaanites and the Hittites and
the Amorites and the Perizzites and the Hivites
and the Jebusites"* (Exodus 3:6,8).

**B.   What Was the Relationship Between God
        and Israel?**

1.   The relationship between God and Israel
        was a covenant relationship by which Israel
        would become a people holy to God.

*And Moses went up to God, and the Lord called to
him from the mountain, saying, "Thus you shall
say to the house of Jacob, and tell the children of
Israel: 'You have seen what I did to the Egyptians,
and how I bore you on eagles' wings and brought
you to Myself. Now therefore, if you will indeed
obey My voice and keep My covenant, then you
shall be a special treasure to Me above all people;
for all the earth is Mine. And you shall be to Me a
kingdom of priests and a holy nation.' These are*

41

the words which you shall speak to the children of Israel" (Exodus 19:3-6).

2. The relationship between God and Israel was based upon the law that He gave them through Moses at Mount Sinai.

Israel received a summary of God's moral law in the form of Ten Commandments.

C. What Is the Nature and Purpose of the Law God Gave to Israel?

1. The law was a code set forth by God through Moses that represented the heart and character of a holy God.

Therefore, the law is holy, and the commandment holy and just and good (Romans 7:12).

Righteous are You, O Lord, and upright are Your judgments (Psalm 119:137).

2. The law taught Israel about sin and how to live with a holy God.

Therefore by the deeds of the law no flesh will be justified in His sight, for by the law is the knowledge of sin (Romans 3:20).

I was alive once without the law, but when the commandment came, sin revived and I died. And the commandment, which was to bring life, I found to bring death (Romans 7:9-10).

For I through the law died to the law that I might live to God (Galatians 2:19).

3.　　The law was in place to lead us to Christ.

What purpose then does the law serve? It was added because of transgressions, till the Seed should come to whom the promise was made; and it was appointed through angels by the hand of a mediator (Galatians 3:19).

But before faith came, we were kept under guard by the law, kept for the faith which would afterward be revealed. Therefore the law was our tutor to bring us to Christ, that we might be justified by faith. But after faith has come, we are no longer under a tutor (Galatians 3:23-25).

For what the law could not do in that it was weak through the flesh, God did by sending His own Son in the likeness of sinful flesh, on account of sin: He condemned sin in the flesh (Romans 8:3).

4.　　The law was in man's heart from the very beginning.

For when Gentiles, who do not have the law, by nature do the things in the law, these, although not having the law, are a law to themselves, who show the work of the law written in their hearts, their conscience also bearing witness, and between themselves their thoughts accusing or else excusing them (Romans 2:14-15).

D.　What Are the Ten Commandments and What Do They Teach Us? What Do They Forbid?

1.　　The first commandment is: You shall have no other gods before Me (Exodus 20:3).

43

Teaches: There is only one God, and He alone is worthy of our love and worship.

Forbids: We are not to serve or worship other gods, persons, places, or things.

Who is like You, O Lord, among the gods? Who is like You, glorious in holiness, fearful in praises, doing wonders? (Exodus 15:11)

You shall love the Lord your God with all your heart, with all your soul, and with all your strength (Deuteronomy 6:5).

Then Jesus said to him, "Away with you, satan! For it is written, 'You shall worship the Lord your God, and Him only you shall serve' " (Matthew 4:10).

Therefore concerning the eating of things offered to idols, we know that an idol is nothing in the world, and that there is no other God but one (1 Corinthians 8:4).

2.   The second commandment is: You shall not make for yourself a carved image (Exodus 20:4).

Teaches: Our God is Spirit whose likeness and glory cannot be represented by a physical image.

Forbids: We are not to make any other image or idol.

For you shall worship no other god, for the Lord, whose name is Jealous, is a jealous God (Exodus 34:14).

I am the Lord, that is My name; and My glory I will not give to another, nor My praise to carved images (Isaiah 42:8).

3.   The third commandment is: You shall not take the name of the Lord your God in vain (Exodus 20:7).

Teaches: We are to speak the name of God with reverence as we call upon Him in prayer and worship.

Forbids: We are not to use the name of God lightly or in cursing or swearing or in any way that does not serve His purpose.

And you shall not swear by My name falsely, nor shall you profane the name of your God: I am the Lord (Leviticus 19:12).

But above all, my brethren, do not swear, either by heaven or by earth or with any other oath. But let your "Yes," be "Yes," and your "No," "No," lest you fall into judgment (James 5:12).

4.   The fourth commandment is: Remember the Sabbath day, to keep it holy (Exodus 20:8).

Teaches: The Sabbath as a religious observance was abolished along with other holy days and ritual observances. Our Sabbath rest is now in Christ. Early Christians met on the first day of the week. This was referred to as the "Lord's Day." We as Christians gather to celebrate Christ, not to fulfill an obligation.

And He said to them, "The Sabbath was made for man, and not man for the Sabbath. Therefore the Son of Man is also Lord of the Sabbath" (Mark 2:27-28).

Yet I say to you that in this place there is One greater than the temple. But if you had known what this means, "I desire mercy and not sacrifice," you would not have condemned the guiltless. For the Son of Man is Lord even of the Sabbath (Matthew 12:6-8).

Now on the first day of the week, when the disciples came together to break bread, Paul, ready to depart the next day, spoke to them and continued his message until midnight (Acts 20:7).

On the first day of the week let each one of you lay something aside, storing up as he may prosper, that there be no collections when I come (1 Corinthians 16:2).

So let no one judge you in food or in drink, or regarding a festival or a new moon or sabbaths, which are a shadow of things to come, but the substance is of Christ (Colossians 2:16-17).

For we who have believed do enter that rest, as He has said: "So I swore in My wrath, 'They shall not enter My rest,'" although the works were finished from the foundation of the world...There remains therefore a rest for the people of God. For he who has entered His rest has himself also ceased from his works as God did from His (Hebrews 4:3,9-10).

5.   The fifth commandment is, Honor your father and your mother, that your days may be long upon the land which the Lord your God is giving you (Exodus 20:12).

Teaches: We are to respect and obey our parents and those in authority. We understand that God is the one who has established authority over us.

Submitting yourselves one to another in the fear of God. Wives, submit yourselves unto your own husbands, as unto the Lord (Ephesians 5:21-22 KJV).

Children, obey your parents in the Lord: for this is right...Servants, be obedient to them that are your masters according to the flesh, with fear and trembling, in singleness of your heart, as unto Christ...And, ye masters, do the same things unto them, forbearing threatening: knowing that your

Master also is in heaven; neither is there respect of persons with Him (Ephesians 6:1,5,9 KJV).

Let every soul be subject unto the higher powers. For there is no power but of God: the powers that be are ordained of God (Romans 13:1 KJV).

Be kindly affectioned one to another with brotherly love; in honour preferring one another (Romans 12:10 KJV).

Forbids: We are not to be rebellious or disobedient against parents and others in authority of any kind, including civil authority.

Render therefore to all their due: taxes to whom taxes are due, customs to whom customs, fear to whom fear, honor to whom honor. Owe no one anything except to love one another, for he who loves another has fulfilled the law (Romans 13:7-8).

6.   The sixth commandment is: You shall not murder (Exodus 20:13).

Teaches: All human life is sacred and precious, including that of the unborn. God has not given us the power of life and death over others. We are to preserve life, especially the innocent and those in need.

Defend the poor and fatherless: do justice to the afflicted and needy. Deliver the poor and needy: rid them out of the hand of the wicked (Psalm 82:3-4 KJV).

But when they persecute you in this city, flee ye into another: for verily I say unto you, Ye shall not have gone over the cities of Israel, till the Son of man be come (Matthew 10:23 KJV).

For no one ever hated his own flesh, but nourishes and cherishes it, just as the Lord does the church (Ephesians 5:29).

Forbids: We are not to take the life of another or ourselves. That is God's right alone. Anger or cursing another person is the same as murder.

Whoever sheds man's blood, by man his blood shall be shed; for in the image of God He made man (Genesis 9:6).

But I say to you that whoever is angry with his brother without a cause shall be in danger of the judgment. And whoever says to his brother, "Raca!" shall be in danger of the council. But whoever says, "You fool!" shall be in danger of hell fire (Matthew 5:22).

Whoever hates his brother is a murderer, and you know that no murderer has eternal life abiding in him (1 John 3:15).

7. The seventh commandment is: You shall not commit adultery (Exodus 20:14).

Teaches: Marriage is a covenant made before God and God's plan for the home. We are to live pure lives, not provoking others or ourselves to sexual sin by what we say or do.

That every one of you should know how to possess his vessel in sanctification and honour; not in the lust of concupiscence, even as the Gentiles which know not God (1 Thessalonians 4:4-5 KJV).

Nevertheless, to avoid fornication, let every man have his own wife, and let every woman have her own husband (1 Corinthians 7:2 KJV)

But I say unto you, That whosoever looketh on a woman to lust after her hath committed adultery with her already in his heart (Matthew 5:28 KJV).

Let no corrupt communication proceed out of your mouth, but that which is good to the use of edifying, that it may minister grace unto the hearers (Ephesians 4:29 KJV).

Let your speech always be with grace, seasoned with salt, that you may know how you ought to answer each one (Colossians 4:6).

Forbids:　We are not to have any kind of sexual relations outside of marriage. This includes all impure and unclean thoughts or desires. Marriage is intended to be a lifelong union between one man and one woman, not broken by anything but death.

But fornication and all uncleanness or covetousness, let it not even be named among you, as is fitting for saints; neither filthiness, nor foolish talking, nor coarse jesting, which are not fitting, but rather giving of thanks (Ephesians 5:3-4).

8.　　The eighth commandment is: You shall not steal (Exodus 20:15).

Teaches: We are to gain wealth and advance without taking advantage of other people. We should respect the property of other people. Our finances are a witness of our relationship with the Lord.

Be diligent to know the state of your flocks, and attend to your herds (Proverbs 27:23).

If one of your brethren becomes poor, and falls into poverty among you, then you shall help him, like a stranger or a sojourner, that he may live with you (Leviticus 25:35).

The soul of a lazy man desires, and has nothing; but the soul of the diligent shall be made rich (Proverbs 13:4).

For even when we were with you, we commanded you this: If anyone will not work, neither shall he eat. For we hear that there are some who walk among you in a disorderly manner, not working at all, but are busybodies. Now those who are such we command and exhort through our Lord Jesus Christ that they work in quietness and eat their own bread (2 Thessalonians 3:10-12).

Forbids: We are not to take the property of other people or defraud anyone in any way of what belongs to them. This includes any kind of business we conduct.

But if anyone does not provide for his own, and especially for those of his household, he has denied the faith and is worse than an unbeliever (1 Timothy 5:8).

Let him who stole steal no longer, but rather let him labor, working with his hands what is good, that he may have something to give him who has need (Ephesians 4:28).

Getting treasures by a lying tongue is the fleeting fantasy of those who seek death (Proverbs 21:6).

9. The ninth commandment is: You shall not bear false witness against your neighbor (Exodus 20:16).

Teaches: We are to avoid any type of lying, falsehood, and slander against our neighbors or anyone else. We must speak the truth and speak only those things which build up.

A false witness will not go unpunished, and he who speaks lies will not escape (Proverbs 19:5).

And above all things have fervent love for one another, for "love will cover a multitude of sins" (1 Peter 4:8).

Forbids: Do not lie to or about anyone. We must not say anything that harms his good name in any way.

Judge not, and you shall not be judged. Condemn not, and you shall not be condemned. Forgive, and you will be forgiven (Luke 6:37).

Do not speak evil of one another, brethren. He who speaks evil of a brother and judges his brother, speaks evil of the law and judges the law. But if you judge the law, you are not a doer of the law but a judge (James 4:11).

10.   The tenth commandment is: You shall not covet your neighbor's house...nor anything that is your neighbor's (Exodus 20:17).

Teaches: We should be content with what we have and charitable to others. Our attitude should be filled with holy desires toward others and we should rejoice in their blessings.

Rejoice with those who rejoice, and weep with those who weep (Romans 12:15).

Let each of you look out not only for his own interests, but also for the interests of others (Philippians 2:4).

Delight yourself also in the Lord, and He shall give you the desires of your heart (Psalm 37:4).

Love suffers long and is kind; love does not envy; love does not parade itself, is not puffed up; does not behave rudely, does not seek its own, is not provoked, thinks no evil; does not rejoice in iniquity, but rejoices in the truth (1 Corinthians 13:4-6).

Forbids: We are not to be envious of anything that belongs to anyone else.

Let your conduct be without covetousness; be content with such things as you have. For He Himself has said, "I will never leave you nor forsake you" (Hebrews 13:5).

And having food and clothing, with these we shall be content. But those who desire to be rich fall into temptation and a snare, and into many foolish and harmful lusts which drown men in destruction and perdition. For the love of money is a root of all kinds of evil, for which some have strayed from the faith in their greediness, and pierced themselves through with many sorrows (1 Timothy 6:8-10).

E.   What Is the Summary of the Ten Commandments?

1.   The first five commandments, or table of the law, deal with our relationship with God.

Then one of them, a lawyer, asked Him a question, testing Him, and saying, "Teacher, which is the great commandment in the law?" Jesus said to him, "You shall love the Lord your God with all your heart, with all your soul, and with all your mind. This is the first and great commandment" (Matthew 22:35-38).

2.   The last five commandments, or second table, deal with our relationship with other people.

And the second is like it: "You shall love your neighbor as yourself." On these two commandments hang all the Law and the Prophets (Matthew 22:39-40).

3.   The summary of all the law is love—love for God and love for man.

Owe no one anything except to love one another, for he who loves another has fulfilled the law. Love does no harm to a neighbor; therefore love is the fulfillment of the law (Romans 13:8,10).

F.   What Are the Results of Not Keeping the Law?

1.   The result of not keeping the law is separation from God and a curse.

Those who depend on obeying the Law live under a curse. For the scripture says, "Whoever does not always obey everything that is written in the book of the Law is under God's curse!" (Galatians 3:10 TEV).

2.   No man can be saved by keeping the law. We are saved by grace through faith alone.

Now, it is clear that no one is put right with God by means of the Law, because the scripture says, "Only the person who is put right with God through faith shall live" (Galatians 3:11 TEV).

3.   No man can keep the law perfectly. But Christ took upon Himself the curse of the law so that we might inherit the blessings God promised to Abraham. Jesus was the only one ever born who walked in perfect faith and obedience.

But by becoming a curse for us Christ has redeemed us from the curse that the Law brings; for the scripture says, "Anyone who is hanged on a tree is under God's curse." Christ did this in order that the blessing which God promised to Abraham might be given to the Gentiles by means of Christ Jesus, so that through faith we might receive the Spirit promised by God (Galatians 3:13-14 TEV).

G. **How Did God Confirm His Covenant Relationship With Israel?**

1. God spoke to Moses on Mount Sinai to establish His covenant and law with Israel.

And Moses went up to God, and the Lord called to him from the mountain, saying, "Thus you shall say to the house of Jacob, and tell the children of Israel: 'You have seen what I did to the Egyptians, and how I bore you on eagles' wings and brought you to Myself. Now therefore, if you will indeed obey My voice and keep My covenant, then you shall be a special treasure to Me above all people; for all the earth is Mine. And you shall be to Me a kingdom of priests and a holy nation.' These are the words which you shall speak to the children of Israel." So Moses came and called for the elders of the people, and laid before them all these words which the Lord commanded him (Exodus 19:3-7).

2. Moses read all the words of the law to the people of Israel.

Then he took the Book of the Covenant and read in the hearing of the people. And they said, "All that the Lord has said we will do, and be obedient."

And Moses took the blood, sprinkled it on the people, and said, "This is the blood of the covenant which the Lord has made with you according to all these words" (Exodus 24:7-8).

H. Was Israel Able to Keep the Law and Covenant of God?

1. Israel was never able to keep the law and the covenant with God. If man was going to be in relationship with God it would not be by the Old Covenant. God announced through the prophets that He would initiate a New Covenant.

Behold, the days are coming, says the Lord, when I will make a new covenant with the house of Israel and with the house of Judah—not according to the covenant that I made with their fathers in the day that I took them by the hand to lead them out of the land of Egypt, My covenant which they broke, though I was a husband to them, says the Lord (Jeremiah 31:31-32).

2. The New Covenant was not written on stone tablets but in the hearts of the people.

But this is the covenant that I will make with the house of Israel after those days, says the Lord: I will put My law in their minds, and write it on their hearts; and I will be their God, and they shall be My people. No more shall every man teach his neighbor, and every man his brother, saying, "Know the Lord," for they all shall know Me, from the least of them to the greatest of them, says the Lord. For I will forgive their iniquity, and their sin I will remember no more (Jeremiah 31:33-34).

For if that first covenant had been faultless, then no place would have been sought for a second. Because finding fault with them, He says: "Behold, the days are coming, says the Lord, when I will make a new covenant with the house of Israel and with the house of Judah...In that He says, "A new covenant," He has made the first obsolete. Now what is becoming obsolete and growing old is ready to vanish away (Hebrews 8:7-8,13).

Let's Review What We Have Learned About Israel and the Law.

1.   The _____ of Israel grew into the nation of Israel while they lived in the land of _____ for over 400 years.

2.   God wanted to continue His _____ with the nation of _____ by bringing them into what He had promised to Abraham.

3.   The relationship between God and Israel was based upon the _____ that He gave them through _____ at Mount Sinai.

4.   The law taught Israel about _____ and how to _____ with a holy God.

5.   *Therefore the law was our tutor to bring us to Christ, that we might be justified by faith* (Galatians 3:24).

6.   How many of the Ten Commandments can you list?

_____

_____

_____

_____

_____

_____

_____

7.   The summary of all the law is _____ for God and for man.

8.   Since Israel was never able to keep the covenant that God had given to them, what kind of covenant did He announce through the prophet Jeremiah?

_____

9.   According to Jeremiah 31, where would God write His New Covenant?

_____

_____

10. Who was the only one who could ever walk in perfect faith and obedience to the Father? _____

Dig a Little Deeper; Grow a Little Closer

1. Read and respond to the following Scripture.

   *By faith Abraham **obeyed** when he was called to go out to the place which he would **receive** as an inheritance. And he went out, not knowing where he was going. By faith he **dwelt** in the land of promise as in a foreign country, dwelling in tents with Isaac and Jacob, the heirs with him of the same promise; for he **waited** for the city which has foundations, whose builder and maker is God* (Hebrews 11:8-10).

2. List all the things in this passage that Abraham did because of his faith/trust in God.

   _____

   _____

   _____

   _____

3. There are times when God is calling us to trust Him. Of the things you named above that Abraham did by faith/trust in God, where do you struggle the most? After you have listed those areas, pray and submit them to the Lord.

   _____

   _____

   _____

   _____

Review Notes

_____

_____

_____

_____

_____

_____

_____

_____

_____

_____

_____

_____

_____

_____

_____

_____

_____

_____

_____

_____

_____

_____

Israel, Called to Be the People of God

_____

_____

_____

_____

_____

_____

_____

_____

_____

_____

_____

_____

_____

_____

_____

_____

_____

_____

_____

_____

_____

_____

_____

_____

_____

_____

_____

Israel, Called to Be the People of God

Israel, Called to Be the People of God

Israel, Called to Be the People of God

A Call to Faith and Obedience

_____

_____

_____

_____

_____

_____

_____

_____

_____

_____

_____

_____

_____

_____

_____

_____

_____

_____

_____

_____

_____

_____

_____

_____

_____

Israel, Called to Be the People of God

A Call to Faith and Obedience

Israel, Called to Be the People of God

Be sure to journal in this book how God responds to what you have prayed.

_____

_____

_____

_____

_____

_____

_____

_____

_____

_____

_____

_____

_____

_____

_____

_____

_____

_____

_____

_____

Books in the *Laying the FOUNDATION* Series

Book 1—The Nature of God

    I.   The Nature of God

    II.   The Bible

    III.   The Creation

Book 2—The Nature of Man

    I.   The Nature of Man

    II.   The Fall of Man

    III.   The Seed of Rebellion Continues

Book 3—A Call to Faith and Obedience

    I.   Abraham: The Father of Fatih and Obedience

    II.   Israel: Called to be the People of God

Book 4—From Covenant to Kingdom

    I.   Taking Possession of the Promises of God

    II.   Establishing the Kingdom

    III.   The Message of the Prophets

    IV.   Restoring the Remnant of Israel

Book 5—The New Covenant

    I.   The New Covenant

    II.   The Person of Jesus Christ

    III.   The Nature of Jesus Christ

    IV.   The Humiliation of Jesus Christ

More Titles
by Dr. Mark Hanby

➤ **YOU HAVE NOT MANY FATHERS**

"My son, give me your heart." So says the proverb, echoing the heart and passion of our Father in heaven. God has spiritual "dads" all over the world whom He has filled with wisdom, knowledge, compassion, and most of all, love for those young in the faith. You do not have to go through your life untrained and unloved; uncared for and forgotten. There are fathers in Christ who are waiting to pour all they have into your heart, as Elijah did for Elisha. "My son, give me your heart."
ISBN 1-56043-166-0

➤ **YOU HAVE NOT MANY FATHERS STUDY GUIDE**

ISBN 0-7684-2036-9

➤ **THE HOUSE THAT GOD BUILT**

Beyond whatever man can desire is a God-given pattern for the life of the Church. Here Dr. Hanby unfolds practical applications from the design of the Tabernacle that allow us to become the house God is building today.
ISBN 1-56043-091-5

➤ **THE HOUSE THAT GOD BUILT STUDY GUIDE**

ISBN 0-7684-2048-2

➤ **THE RENEWING OF THE HOLY GHOST**

Do you need renewal? Everything in the natural, from birds to blood cells, must either undergo a process of renewal or enter into death. Our spiritual life is no different. With this book, your renewal can begin today!
ISBN 1-56043-031-1

➤ **ANOINTING THE UNSANCTIFIED**

The anointing is more than a talented performance or an emotional response. In this book, Dr. Hanby details the essential ingredients of directional relationship that allow the Spirit of God to flow down upon the Body of Christ—and from us to the needs of a dying world.
ISBN 1-56043-071-0

➤ **PERCEIVING THE WHEEL OF GOD**

On the potter's wheel, a lump of clay yields to a necessary process of careful pressure and constant twisting. Similarly, the form of true faith is shaped by a trusting response to God in a suffering situation. This book offers essential understanding for victory through the struggles of life.
ISBN 1-56043-109-1

Available at your local Christian bookstore.

For more information and sample chapters, visit www.destinyimage.com